ERO WASTE

BY ECOBOOKS
DESIGNED IN BARCELONA 2020

THIS NOTEBOOK BELONGS TO:

_____

YEAR

2021

Waste isn't waste
Until
We waste it

ZERO WASTE

What is Zero waste? It is a philosophy that encourages the redesign of resource life cycles so that all products are reused. The goal is for no trash to be sent to landfills, incinerators, or the ocean.

ONLY 9% OF PLASTIC IS ACTUALLY RECYCLED.

"Zero Waste is a goal that is both pragmatic and visionary, to guide people to emulate sustainable natural cycles, where all discarded materials are resources for others to use. Zero Waste means designing and managing products and processes to reduce the volume and toxicity of waste and materials, conserve and recover all resources, and not burn or bury them. Implementing Zero Waste will eliminate all discharges to land, water, or air that may be a threat to planetary, human, animal, or plant health." Definition of Zero Waste as adopted by the Zero Waste International Alliance.

According to some estimates, if we continue on our current path,

THE OCEANS WILL CONTAIN MORE PLASTIC THAN FISH BY THE YEAR 2050.

We've produced as much plastic in the past decade as we did in the entire twentieth century. We're drowning in the stuff, and we need to start making some hard choices. The principles of zero waste lifestyle are simple, which are waste prevention, separate collection, and reduction of residual waste. For waste prevention, the consumer is suggested to purchase only goods which are needed and eliminate the use of one time disposal products, while industrial and firm should produce long lifespan and repairable products using recycled materials together with minimum and recyclable packaging in order to phase out waste.

A zero-waste lifestyle means to send nothing to a landfill. We reduce what we need, reuse as much as we can, send little to be recycled, and compost what we cannot. It's about redefining the system.

We live in a linear economy where we take resources from the earth and then dump them in the ocean. The goal of zero waste is to move to a circular economy where we write trash out of existence.

THE CIRCULAR ECONOMY MIMICS NATURE IN THAT THERE IS NO TRASH IN NATURE.

Thinking about the waste we generate is a critical step in moving towards a more sustainable way of life.

Both when at home, and when traveling, it is important to consider the waste we create, and to reduce it as much as possible.

We should take measures to get as close as possible to a zero waste lifestyle, eliminating waste in all its forms.

The major areas for waste reduction are: food, water, energy, packaging & plastic waste Focusing on these areas can help us to move towards zero waste lifestyle.

Zero food waste

Ridiculous amounts of food are thrown away each year. We can all reduce food waste by:

- Choosing Restaurants which grow food and compost their own waste.
- Taking a list shopping and not over-buying
- Asking for a 'doggy bag' to save any leftovers when dining out.
- Having a zero waste kitchen.

Zero water waste

We can also reduce water waste by:

- Switching off taps while brushing our teeth.
- Using the plugin sinks or shower-baths to save the water.
- Taking fewer, shorter baths and showers.

Zero energy waste

We can help reduce energy waste by:

- Switching off lights/ heating/ air conditioning when we do not need them.
- Reducing the number of electrical gadgets we use.
- Choosing low-energy or self-powered means of transportation to get around.

Reducing Packaging & plastic waste

We can reduce the plastic and landfill waste we generate by:

- Selecting to shop at markets for fresh produce rather than buying packaged.
- Taking reusable drinks bottles with us

We must all embrace fundamental changes in the way we live our lives. But it can be easy to become overwhelmed. It can be easy to throw up our hands and ask what exactly we as individuals, can really do.

If you are looking for motivation to reduce waste and your footprint on our precious earth this planner is for you!

If you are trying to transition into an eco-friendly lifestyle, this journal will help you along the way.

This is your year to save the planet. What are you waiting for?

Questions to ask myself before buying something:

–Do I have any substitute of this?

– Is it reusable?

– Does it put my family's health in danger?

– Do I keep it because society tells me that I need one?

– Does it truly help me?

– Could something else achieve the same task?

There are many books that explain why not to use plastic or to have a zero-waste life, but the truth is that none of those books actually get you into action. This planner is made for you to start changing the world from today.

The cautionary tale of the boiling frog describes how a frog that jumps into boiling water will save itself by jumping straight out, but the frog that sits in the water while it gradually gets hotter and hotter will boil to death. The global warming crisis surrounds us today and we must act now to protect ourselves..

Source: www.unep.org

IN THIS BOOK, YOU WILL FIND:

1. Useful information about zero waste and climate change

2. Guided templates to fill with your zero waste plan for:
- Beauty
- Kitchen
- Bathroom
- Cleaning
- Eco gifts
- Clothes
- Christmas time
- Books and blogs
- Party decorations
- Shops
- Travel
- Plastic counter and more!

3. Tips on how to have a zero waste lifestyle

4. Zero waste habit tracker

5. Monthly planner

6. Weekly planner – undated so it can be used at any time in the future

7- Pages to write down your Zero waste recipes

8- Garden notes

A HISTORY OF THE PLASTIC SHOPPING BAG

A rare novelty in the 1970s, plastic shopping bags are now an omnipresent global product, produced at a rate of one trillion a year. They are showing up in the darkest depths of the oceans to the summit of Mount Everest to the polar ice caps – and creating some major environmental challenges.
How did this happen?

1933 – Polyethylene, the most commonly used plastic, is created by accident at a chemical plant in Northwich, England. While polyethylene had been created in small batches before, this was the first synthesis of the material that was industrially practical, and it was initially used in secret by the British military during World War II.

1965 – The one-piece polyethylene shopping bag is patented by the Swedish company Celloplast. Designed by engineer Sten Gustaf Thulin, the plastic bag quickly begins to replace cloth and plastic in Europe.

1979 – Already controlling 80% of the bag market in Europe, plastic bags go abroad and are widely introduced to the United States. Plastic companies begin to aggressively market their product as superior to paper and reusable bags.

1982 – Safeway and Kroger, two of the biggest supermarket chains in the United States, switch to plastic bags. More stores follow suit and by the end of the decade plastic bags will have almost replaced paper around the world.

1982 – Safeway and Kroger, two of the biggest supermarket chains in the United States, switch to plastic bags. More stores follow suit and by the end of the decade plastic bags will have almost replaced paper around the world.

1997 – Sailor and researcher Charles Moore discovers the Great Pacific Garbage Patch, the largest of several gyres in the world's oceans where immense amounts of plastic waste have accumulated, threatening marine life. Plastic bags are notorious for killing sea turtles, which mistakenly think they are jellyfish and eat them.

2002 – Bangladesh is the first country in the world to implement a ban on thin plastic bags, after it was found they played a key role in clogging drainage systems during disastrous flooding. Other countries begin to follow suit.

2011 – Worldwide one million plastic bags are consumed every minute.

2017 – Kenya bans plastic bags, making it one the most recent of the more than two dozen countries that have sought to reduce plastic bag use through fees or bans.

2018 – #BeatPlasticPollution is chosen as the theme of World Environment Day. Companies and governments around the world continue to announce new pledges to tackle plastic waste.

Source: www.unep.org

Every straw counts in the fight against climate change

The word "Mottainai" in Japanese literally translates to "it is a shame to waste." It stems from Buddhist philosophy on living minimally and appreciating nature's gifts. The practice has been in place for generations.

Japan is often heralded as having one of the most sophisticated recycling systems in the world, with detailed separation of everything from radios to cat litter.

Straws seem a small part of the equation, but if each person in Asia were to use a plastic straw on a given day, it would mean 4.5 billion straws making their way into the waste system.

Urban population in developing nations is projected to continue to grow, adding 2.5 billion people to the world's cities by 2050, By then, more than half of the world's population will live in cities.

A key step to managing rapid urbanization, reducing poverty and addressing equity and environmental issues amongst urban residents is to meet their needs for access to services and opportunities. Walking and cycling are more than low-carbon modes of transport that enhance urban quality and facilitate social cohesion. They are cheap, flexible, personal modes without which most people in low- and middle-income countries would be unable to participate in the economy and community, or access education, healthcare and other urban services.

Cycling leads to a longer and healthier life

Cycling has become popular for a variety of reasons. It helps to reduce the risk of diabetes, some forms of cancer, cardiovascular diseases and depression. The health benefits of cycling daily rather than taking a car for short trips outweigh the risks of Inhalation of air pollutants. Daily exercise prolongs life expectancy by approximately 3.4 years whereas inhalation of polluted air reduces life expectancy by 1 to 40 days. Regular cycling boosts physical fitness and is an efficient way to prevent obesity.

Cycling, the better mode of transport

Cycling saves money Cycling is a cheap mode of transport. The annual costs of cycling range from US$200 to US$340. By comparison, the costs involved in driving a car range from US$2,800 to US$9,600 euros a year.

Source: www.unep.org

Clean air as a human right

If you live in a high-income country, you have about a one in two chance of breathing in air that exceeds World Health Organization guidelines for air pollution. That's worrying enough, but if you live in a city in a low- or middle-income country, the chances of breathing in clean air are much slimmer still

Most of the global population is exposed without their consent to hazardous substances and wastes that increase their likelihood of developing diseases and disabilities throughout their lives. In some cases, it has the potential to be a human rights violation.

The World Health Organization estimates that 23 per cent of all deaths worldwide—a total to 12.6 million people in 2012—are exposed to environmental risks. Low- and middle-income countries bear the brunt of pollution-related illnesses, with a disproportionate impact on children, women and the most vulnerable. Air pollution alone kills an estimated seven million people worldwide every year.

What would the world look like if the enjoyment of a healthy environment was indeed universally recognized as a fundamental human right?

While chemicals contribute to our everyday development, the unsound management of chemicals and waste can create dangerous sources of pollution for our societies and environment.

This means that everybody must have access to environmental information.

Placing human rights at the core of environmental issues would be beneficial for everyone, no matter what their job is or what city they live in. We would all benefit from cleaner air, water and soil, as will the generations that come after us. Ensuring that the most vulnerable people in society are protected will ensure the protection of the entire global community.

Source: www.unep.org

Smartphones have revolutionized our daily lives. From instant messaging to global interaction at our fingertips, today's communication is fast, efficient and low-cost.

But how smart are our phones when it comes to the impact on the environment?

Gold, silver, cobalt, tin, tantalum, tungsten and copper are all essential components of mobile phones and other electrical devices we use daily. And, since mining is one of the most intensive users of heavy fuel oil, extraction contributes significantly to climate change.

Beyond carbon footprint, the biggest environmental concern where e-waste is concerned is the impact at the end of a product's life. Yet, around 80 per cent of the carbon footprint of a smartphone occurs during the manufacturing process, with 16 per cent down to consumer use and 3 per cent accounted for by transport.

And as demand for smartphones rises, the lifespan of devices shrinks. Increasingly sophisticated smart phones are discarded. Tough competition drives mobile companies to produce the next, best, latest, thinner and smarter phone.

Product lifetime is getting shorter and shorter, thus less sustainable

The fast replacement rate of smartphones due to technical development and market strategy is unsustainable, often generating unnecessary waste of fully-functioning devices

Making our phones truly smart not only entails recycling, upcycling and repurposing materials that go into them. But also, building them to last: reducing our phone footprint and designing sustainable models which make waste in the long term a thing of the past.

Is your phone really smart?

Source: www.unep.org

The hidden plastics in your beauty products

Go into any beauty store and you will see shelves full of products that promise to fix every problem with your appearance that you didn't realize you had.

Many people are not aware of just how much plastic is hidden in their beauty routine.

Take a look at your bathroom. At first glance you may notice the plastic used to package your shampoo, make-up, shower gel, and almost every personal care product you own.

At second glance, you may start to pay attention to the everyday plastic products that you have always used without consideration of their plastic footprint—your toothbrush, your razor, your disposable face wipes and your cotton buds.

But not all plastic is visible to the naked eye. Whilst microplastics are any piece of plastic under 5 mm in size, microbeads are a type of microplastic smaller than 1 mm. Even smaller than that are nanoplastics, which are so small that they can pass through human skin.

Microplastics are intentionally added to all kinds of products and not limited to exfoliants. Products that contain plastic polymers are deodorant, shampoo, conditioner, shower gel, lipstick, hair dye, shaving cream, sunscreen, insect repellent, anti-wrinkle cream, moisturizers, hair spray, facial masks, baby care products, eye shadow, mascara and more. In some cases, these products are made of more than 90 per cent plastic.

Plastic ingredients are so prevalent because they can be added for the following functions: skin conditioning, exfoliants, abrasives, glitter, tooth polishing, viscosity regulators to make the products flow, emulsifiers, film formers, opacifying agents, liquid absorbents binders, bulking agents, and more.

Microplastics in personal care products can go effortlessly down the drain as you wash. Because they are so small, wastewater filtration cannot treat them, and they can easily enter rivers and seas.

Since microplastics are not biodegradable, when in the sea they attract waterborne toxins and bacteria that stick to their shiny surface and look similar to food items. They can then be eaten by fish, amphibians, insects, larvae and marine animals. Plastics can block digestive tracts, or enter the food chain where they may eventually end up on our dinner plates.

The health impact of microplastics on humans is not fully known and more research is needed to understand their effect on our bodies.

Sustainable, ocean-friendly alternatives are available, and by demanding plastic-free products and materials, the industry will have to respond. Switch to plastic-free packaging where possible, pledge to stop using products that contain hidden plastics, and demand change from the beauty brands that use them excessively.

Source: www.unep.org

FACTS

Plastic

• Globally only 9% of plastic ever produced has been recycled, while 79% can now be found in landfills, dumps or the environment and 12% has been incinerated.

• It takes 500 years for average sized plastic water bottles to fully decompose.

• Over 100,000 marine animals die every year from plastic entanglement and ingestion.

• Humans now buy a million plastic bottles a minute. Most of this plastic ends up in the ocean. By 2050, the ocean will contain more plastic by weight than fish.

• In 2015 almost 50% of the plastic waste generated globally was single-use packaging. If continued at the same rate, the plastic industry will account for 20% of the world's total oil consumption by 2050.

Water

• Less than 3 percent of the world's water is fresh (drinkable), of which 2.5 percent is frozen in Antarctica, Arctic, and glaciers.

• Humankind is polluting water in rivers and lakes faster than nature can recycle and purify.

• More than 1 billion people still do not have access to fresh water.

Climate:

From 1880 to 2012, the average global temperature increased by 0.85ºC.

For each 1 degree of temperature increase, grain yields decline by about 5 percent. Oceans have warmed, the amounts of snow and ice have diminished, and sea level has risen.

If we don´t take action climate change will cause average global temperatures to increase beyond 3ºC.

Energy

The world's cities occupy just 3 percent of the Earth's land but account for 60-80 percent of energy consumption and 75 percent of carbon emissions.

Roughly 1 billion people (13% of the world's population) live without electricity with around 118 million people gaining access to electricity each year.

1/3 all food goes to waste

Reference: National geographics / United Nations

Every small step matters when it comes to reducing plastic waste. Start Today!

Be part of the solution,
not part of the pollution.

MY ZERO WASTE LISTS

Moving towards a zero waste lifestyle often begins in the kitchen. And the kitchen is certainly a good place to start. Much of the plastic waste that comes into our homes is brought in with the food that we buy. Plastic also accumulates in kitchens surrounding food prep and food storage.

Reducing Plastic Waste in the Kitchen

To reduce plastic waste in your kitchen, your first step should be to reduce the amount of food that you buy. Growing at least some of your own food is one of the best steps you can take to move to a more sustainable way of life. To cut down on single use plastic, you can also:

❖ Shop with a list to avoid overbuying.

❖ Take a reusable bag with you to the shops.

❖ Shop in a farm shop, wholesaler or zero waste store whenever possible.

❖ Buy fresh, seasonal and ideally organic ingredients, sourced as locally as possible. Cook from scratch rather than buying pre-processed and heavily packaged foods.

❖ Use beeswax wraps or silicone, glass or metal containers to store food, rather than plastic wrap or plastic containers.

❖ Choose wooden rather than plastic cooking utensils.

❖ Avoid using disposable plates or cutlery, or if you must use them, choosing sustainable options such as those made from bamboo instead of plastic.

❖ Choose stainless steel, copper, iron or ceramic cookware rather than Teflon coated non-recyclable non-stick pans.

You can also reduce food waste in your kitchen by saving leftovers, growing vegetables from scraps and composting.

KITCHEN

Instead of using this

_____
_____
_____
_____
_____
_____
_____
_____
_____
_____
_____
_____
_____
_____
_____
_____

Now I'm using this

_____
_____
_____
_____
_____
_____
_____
_____
_____
_____
_____
_____
_____
_____
_____
_____

If we are not careful, our bathrooms can fill up with all sorts of plastic and non-recyclable products. Fortunately, there are plenty of great solutions out there to help you cut waste in your bathroom. For example, to move towards zero waste living you should:

❖ Adopt a 'no poo' approach to your haircare. Wash with natural ingredients (such as bicarbonate of soda and apple cider vinegar, natural Castile soap and botanicals). This will help limit or even eliminate plastic bottles from your bathroom.

❖ Choose a natural loofah or sponge for your bath or shower.

❖ Make your own soaps, cleansers, moisturizers, bath bombs etc using natural ingredients.

❖ Make your own reusable wet wipes using organic, sustainable materials, or buy biodegradable, plastic free ones.

❖ Choose a bamboo or wooden toothbrush with natural bristles.

❖ Use tooth powder or paste that comes in jars or metal tins rather than in plastic tubes. (Or make your own).

❖ Choose natural silk floss or natural tooth picks to avoid nylon floss. (But make sure it comes from an ethical source.)

❖ Opt for organic cotton buds with wood or bamboo rather than plastic.

❖ Buy a wooden hair brush with natural bristles.

❖ Choose rubber and organic cotton hair elastics, or use other inventive ways to tie up your hair that don't involve synthetic, non-recyclable materials.

❖ Source wooden-handled, reusable safety razors and wooden shaving brushes with natural bristles.

❖ Women – buy a silicone cup to avoid the use of harmful and polluting sanitary products.

❖ Source sustainable toilet paper without plastic packaging.

BATHROOM

Instead of using this

Now I'm using this

Giving eco-friendly gifts is a great way to encourage others to follow your lead and work towards a zero waste lifestyle. To help you come up with lovely green gift ideas here are a few suggestions:

Gift experiences rather than things

❖ Your time – for example, to help them with a project in their home, with child care, or their garden. Giving them more free time could be the greatest gift of all.

❖ A skill – consider giving the chance to have someone on one time with you to learn a skill. For example, if you are a talented cook – gift a cooking lesson. If you are an artist – gift a one-on-one tutorial.

❖ A tour or excursion. For example, how about gifting a foraging trip, a photography tour, or simply a guided excursion in a beautiful, natural setting. or an activity day.: biking, skiing, horseback riding, etc.

Gift pre-loved or vintage items

If you do wish to gift an object rather than an experience, remember that you do not need to buy new. Pre-loved and vintage items can be just as beautiful as new items, and some just get more appealing with age.

Give gifts that will help others live more sustainably

Think about items you might gift to help them to live more sustainably. For example, you could gift:

❖ Seeds, plants or garden equipment to help them grow their own food.

❖ A tree or other living plant that will help them conserve the environment.

Give things that you have made yourself

A gift that you have made yourself could be far more meaningful than anything you could buy:

❖ Hand-made, natural soaps, bath bombs and other cleaning products.

❖ Knitted or sewed clothing, bags etc..

❖ A unique piece of artwork. (Photography, drawing, sculpture etc..)

ECO GIFTS

Eco-friendly gifts for special occasions

Eco-friendly fashion is about making clothes that take into account the environment, the health of consumers, and the working conditions of people in the fashion industry.

Sustainable fashion is thus partly about producing clothes, shoes, and accessories in an environmentally and socio-economically sustainable manner, but also about more sustainable patterns of consumption and use, which necessitate shifts in individual attitudes and behavior. Fast Fashion is the process of imitating trends and styles from the prominent name designers on the runway. These are often utilized by fashion conscious individuals at a low price.

Although this enables one to access fashion cheaply, it holds a negative effect on the environment and for those creating the garments.

Retail giants exploit their workforce in order to achieve a fast and cheap distribution and high consumption of clothing.

Slow fashion aims to decrease the speed of production, consumption and disposing of by placing greater appreciation on one's purchase. Carefully considering an acquisition, connecting with clothes instead of having just another addition to the wardrobe which may be only worn for one occasion.

- Choose eco-friendly natural materials rather than 'plastic' synthetic fabrics. (Synthetic fabrics are generally less eco-friendly and give off micro-plastics every time they are washed.)

- Choose items from ethical suppliers, who care for the environment and for people at each stage of their production and manufacture. (Look for eco-labels and certifications to help guide your purchases.)

- Choose items that will last, rather than fast, disposable fashion, and consider what will happen to your clothing at the end of its useful life.

The best way to avoid waste is by asking your self if you really need this.

CLOTHES

List of new clothes I buy

Questions to ask myself: Do I really need this? Can I buy it second-hand?
Has this been ethically manufactured?

Date	What	Date	What

Think carefully about whether you really need to wear makeup at all. If you do choose to do so, consider reducing the number of products you purchase and make your own natural makeup instead. For example, make a lip gloss with beeswax, almond oil and essential oils, and mascara from charcoal and aloe vera.

You can also find refillable mascara and lipstick in cardboard packaging and no plastic! Buy ingredients that are sustainably packaged.

On the internet there are many diy recipes. It will depend a lot on your type of skin. It can be a bit of trial and error at first.

If you make something that your skin doesn't like the first time, give it to a friend.

Here some DIY ideas:

Coffee Scrub:

Caffeine contains beneficial antioxidants that can actually reduce cellulite, making it a smart choice for a leg exfoliant.

You'll need 1 cup of coffee, ¾ cup white or brown sugar, ½ cup coconut oil (melted), and ¼ cup olive oil. Mix dry ingredients together first, then add olive, then coconut oil. Once combined, the mixture will take on a crumbly texture. Rub on your legs in gentle, circular motions for anywhere from 2-4 minutes. Rinse off and towel dry.

Avocado Mask:

A mask made for dry skin.

For this recipe, you'll need one skinned, ripe avocado, mashed in a bowl. Then add 1 tablespoon of honey. Apply the paste to the skin and leave it on for 10-15 minutes.

BEAUTY

My Homemade Beauty tricks

_____
_____
_____
_____
_____
_____
_____
_____
_____
_____
_____
_____
_____
_____
_____
_____
_____
_____
_____
_____
_____

One of the most challenging things about moving to a zero waste lifestyle is trying to avoid plastic packaging on things we buy. Buy in bulk and you can move closer to eliminating plastic packaging from your life. But what can you buy in bulk? And how and where can you do so?

Products to buy in bulk

Here are some examples of products that it is sensible to buy in bulk when trying to move towards a zero waste lifestyle:

✓ Food staples, such as rice, pasta, grains and pulses.

✓ Baking ingredients like sugar, flour etc.

✓ Natural soap for household cleaning and your personal natural cleaning regime (such as castile soap).

✓ Bicarbonate of soda (also for cleaning).

✓ Toilet paper.

Of course, there are also a number of other things that you might wish to buy in bulk, depending on what exactly you use on a regular basis. Remember, however, that it is generally better not to overbuy, and to purchase as little as you possibly can.

How and where to buy products in bulk

You can buy food staples in bulk at wholefood stores, which are available now in many towns and cities. Increasingly, zero waste shops are popping up in major settlements. Many allow you to take your own reusable containers with you to collect your goods, to cut down on packaging even more. This link should help you find a bulk location near you. https://app.zerowastehome.com.

You can also often find plastic-free bulk options online. If you are buying in bulk online, try to still find an option based as close to home as possible.

PRODUCTS

List of products that I buy in bulk

Despite transport being the biggest cause of carbon emissions within travel (75%), accommodation makes up for 20% of carbon emissions within travel.

There is a range of things that we should look for when searching for sustainable accommodation. Understanding the issues in sustainability can help us to create a checklist that allows us to see whether or not the options we are considering truly are green, eco-friendly, and truly sustainable choices. Truly sustainable accommodation will take into account:

- energy usage
- water use
- land use (and local environmental conservation)
- materials use
- waste management
- the impact on the local community.

Eco-friendly travel can give us the chance to volunteer our time and skills. It can allow us to head out into the world and lead by example. It can honestly give us opportunities to make our world a better place (while having a wonderful time in the process!).

For example, volunteering may take you:

- To organic farms, where you can help grow food sustainably – learning skills that you could then also implement back home. (World Wide Opportunities on Organic Farms.)
- To help on a range of eco-building projects around the world.
- To rewild areas of natural forest.
- To contribute to conservation projects around the globe.
- To help communities become more self-reliant and work towards a post-carbon economy.

TRAVEL BUCKET LIST

Places to visit and volunteer

_____ _____
_____ _____
_____ _____
_____ _____
_____ _____
_____ _____
_____ _____
_____ _____
_____ _____
_____ _____
_____ _____
_____ _____
_____ _____
_____ _____
_____ _____
_____ _____

Plastic is everywhere. It is something that we use in every element of our lives and has proven a very useful material. Unfortunately, our dependence on plastic also poses a huge, massive problem for our planet. Unlike natural materials, plastic will not biodegrade in the natural environment but sticks around, creating a waste problem of epic proportions. Plastic is now found in every environment on earth – polluting our oceans, waterways, and land, and causing horrendous problems for people and wildlife. The problem of plastic is not an easy one to solve. It will involve a concerted effort from politicians, big business, and individuals. It is easy to become overwhelmed. But we can all do our part to help reduce our impact when it comes to plastic waste. There are plenty of things that we can do to reduce our plastic waste at home,.

Recycling shouldn't be the first line of defense, it should be a last resort.
The best way to reduce our plastic pollution when home, and when out and about is to reduce the amount of plastic that we buy, reuse plastic for as long as possible, and recycle as much as we can. Here are some tips for plastic-free travel:
- Avoid purchasing synthetic clothing/ baggage and other items. Washing these items can release plastic micro-particles into our waterways and oceans.
- Adopt a simple, natural cleaning regime to avoid buying shampoo, conditioners, shower gels, and other toiletries in plastic bottles. (Bicarbonate of soda, apple cider vinegar and a bar of hard natural soap are all you really need).
- Choose products like bamboo toothbrushes, natural wood hair brushes, and other items not made from plastic to take with you on your travels.

PLASTIC COUNTER

Pick a random day and count how many times you use single-use plastic

_____ _____

_____ _____

_____ _____

_____ _____

_____ _____

_____ _____

_____ _____

_____ _____

_____ _____

_____ _____

_____ _____

_____ _____

_____ _____

_____ _____

_____ _____

_____ _____

When it comes to parties there are many sustainable options to decorate your place.

❖ If you choose flowers, try to support a local florist near you, rather than ordering online. It takes less time to get to you, resulting in less carbon emissions. Anyhow most florists source their flowers overseas, so ask your florist where they source them from. When flowers are shipped overseas, they have a huge carbon footprint.

❖ Ask your local florist to omit the floral foam and plastic cellophane wrap when creating your floral designs.

❖ Use colorful displays of fruits, vegetables or even flower petals as table centerpieces.

❖ Look for products that are made with compostable materials. Then, make sure you have clearly marked compost bins so guests can easy help with your efforts.

❖ Choose beeswax candles. Many candles are made with harmful chemicals that are released into the air when we burn them. Beeswax, on the other hand, does not.

❖ Choose cloth napkins, and authentic tableware, glassware and plates, rather than disposables.

❖ Send or text invites digitally instead of printing them on paper. You can even include a little mention of why you chose to send the invites this way.

❖ Make sure you will have clear signage so your guests know where compost and recyclables belong.

❖ keep in mind that glitter and glue will make products unrecyclable.

❖ Avoid balloons. These are bad news for sea turtles.

PARTY DECORATIONS

Ideas of recycled ornaments

_____   _____
_____   _____
_____   _____
_____   _____
_____   _____
_____   _____
_____   _____
_____   _____
_____   _____
_____   _____
_____   _____
_____   _____
_____   _____
_____   _____
_____   _____

What if you no longer feel that "obligation" to give someone anything but feel that you are doing something good by exposing others to why you live the way you do?

Regarding Christmas tree, what if you try ¨Do It Yourself¨. You can create a tree with different objects, such as just recycled paper, fabrics, boxes and more. Have a look at internet for some inspiration.
If you still decide to buy one try to get one small so it is easy to store without taking up space and it is infinitely reusable.

You can opt for homemade nature garlands for an authentic and ecological decoration. A walk in the forest will allow you to find something to make pretty little decorations.
Most of the decorative objects sold everywhere are made in China. Beyond the significant carbon impact linked to the transport from China to the rest of the world, there are toxic paints whose manufacture pollutes and from which organic compounds subsequently emanate.
Advent calendars on the market are made of plastic and offer unhealthy sweets. To overcome this make your own Advent calendar.
Opt for the reverse advent calendar which means is to collect basic necessities or foodstuffs and give them to a person in need or an association.

Regarding food, cook mindfully.
❖ Source locally-grown organic and chemical-free produce
❖ free-range eggs
❖ Sustainably-farmed seafood and avoid meat if possible.

CHRISTMAS TIME!

My holidays plan

_____

_____

_____

_____

_____

_____

_____

_____

_____

_____

_____

_____

_____

_____

_____

_____

_____

_____

_____

_____

How to compost easily at home

Composting organic waste at home is easier than you might imagine. All of us who are trying to live a zero waste lifestyle should compost food scraps and other biodegradable materials at home. Fortunately, if you are new to composting, you will find that it is far easier than you may have imagined.

Composting – the basics

Composting is simply the name given to the process by which organic materials break down over time. In nature, this happens naturally. But in our homes, the main goal is to speed up this process somewhat, and manage the return of nutrients to the system.

There are three main types of composting:

➢ Composting in place.
➢ Cold (aerobic) composting.
➢ Hot (anaerobic) composting.

The first two are the ones that are usually used in a domestic setting.
For these types of composting to take place we need:

▪ Organic material.
▪ Bacteria and other beneficial micro-organisms.
▪ Water.
▪ Oxygen.

The composting process will be better and more efficient when constant and reasonable temperatures are maintained. (Usually between around 10 and 25 degrees.) Composting will still happen in temperatures outside this range, but not as quickly or effectively. Your compost should be kept not too warm and not too cold, not too wet and not too dry. You also need balance when it comes to what you compost. You will need a good mix of what are often referred to as 'green' (nitrogen rich) and 'brown' (carbon rich) materials. Get the balance right, and a good, nutrient rich and fine-textured compost will be the result.

The Easiest Ways to Compost

If you have a garden, you can compost and create new growing areas at the same time. Simply layer brown and green materials on a layer of cardboard on your lawn, top with some compost you source to get you started and plant or sow as you would in an ordinary garden bed. You can also simply make a compost heap or compost bin in the corner of the garden.

If you don't have a garden, the easiest way to compost is in a simple container under your kitchen sink. The process will be easier and quicker if you enlist the help of some special worms. Vermiculture composting is a great way to go where space is limited. You could also look into the idea of a bokashi bucket.

Whichever composting method you choose, as long as you consider the above, you should not go too far wrong.

My compost plan

Take notes of your compost evolution

What I need to get started

Status

_____

_____

_____

_____

_____

_____

_____

_____

_____

_____

_____

_____

_____

_____

_____

_____

EMAILS

Sent to ask companies to save the world: I.e.: to change packaging or to request transparency of ingredients...

Date	To	Request

CLEANING

Homemade cleaning products recipes

_____

_____

_____

_____

_____

_____

_____

_____

_____

_____

_____

_____

_____

_____

_____

_____

_____

_____

_____

_____

LEARN MORE

About living a Zero waste life

Books to read

Blogs to follow

SHOPS

Sustainable shops

Bulk food

Tips on how to live a zero waste life:

- Say no to frozen food and single-serving sizes

- Ask companies to change their packaging

- Choose reusable cloth sandwich/snack bags

- Choose stainless steel ice cube trays and Popsicle molds

- Avoid disposable plastic pens

- Choose pet toys and furniture made from natural materials

- Avoid buying new plastic clothing (polyester, acrylic, lycra)

- Throw a zero-waste party

- Consider giving charitable gift cards

- Grocery shopping with less plastic

- Find ways to wrap gifts without plastic tape

- Request zero plastic packaging when ordering online

- Support small and local businesses

- Buy second-hand

- Use plastic-free food containers

- Explore plastic-free hair accessories

- Bring your own cup

- Say no to plastic straws

- Be a minimalist

- Use a water filter system

- Start your own plastic-free campaign

- Carry reusable shopping bags

- Carry a stainless-steel travel mug

- Treat yourself to an ice cream cone

- Shop at your local farmers market

- Buy fresh bread that comes in either paper bags or no bags

- Buy large wheels of unwrapped cheese

- Clean with vinegar and water

- Use powdered dishwasher detergent in a cardboard box

- Switch to bar soap instead of liquid soap

ZERO WASTE RECIPES

Zero waste recipes

Recipe

SERVING   PREP TIME   COOK TIME   TEMPERATURE

INGREDIENTS

METHODS

LEVEL OF WASTE: ◯ ◯ ◯ ◯ ◯

Zero waste recipes

Recipe

SERVING   PREP TIME   COOK TIME   TEMPERATURE

INGREDIENTS   METHODS

LEVEL OF WASTE: ◯ ◯ ◯ ◯ ◯

ZERO WASTE RECIPES

RECIPE

SERVING	PREP TIME	COOK TIME	TEMPERATURE

INGREDIENTS

_____
_____
_____
_____
_____
_____
_____
_____
_____
_____
_____
_____
_____
_____
_____
_____
_____
_____
_____

METHODS

_____
_____
_____
_____
_____
_____
_____
_____
_____
_____
_____
_____
_____
_____
_____
_____
_____
_____
_____

LEVEL OF WASTE: ◯ ◯ ◯ ◯ ◯

Zero waste recipes

Recipe

SERVING   PREP TIME   COOK TIME   TEMPERATURE

INGREDIENTS   METHODS

LEVEL OF WASTE: ◯ ◯ ◯ ◯ ◯

Zero waste recipes

Recipe

Serving   PrepTime   CookTime   Temperature

Ingredients

_____

_____

_____

_____

_____

_____

_____

_____

_____

_____

_____

_____

_____

_____

_____

_____

_____

_____

_____

_____

_____

Methods

_____

_____

_____

_____

_____

_____

_____

_____

_____

_____

_____

_____

_____

_____

_____

_____

_____

_____

_____

_____

_____

LEVEL OF WASTE: ◯ ◯ ◯ ◯ ◯

ZERO WASTE RECIPES

RECIPE

SERVING   PREP TIME   COOK TIME   TEMPERATURE

INGREDIENTS

_____
_____
_____
_____
_____
_____
_____
_____
_____
_____
_____
_____
_____
_____
_____
_____
_____
_____
_____
_____
_____

METHODS

_____
_____
_____
_____
_____
_____
_____
_____
_____
_____
_____
_____
_____
_____
_____
_____
_____
_____
_____
_____
_____

LEVEL OF WASTE: ◯ ◯ ◯ ◯ ◯

ZERO WASTE RECIPES

RECIPE

SERVING	PREP TIME	COOK TIME	TEMPERATURE

INGREDIENTS

_____

_____

_____

_____

_____

_____

_____

_____

_____

_____

_____

_____

_____

_____

_____

_____

_____

_____

_____

METHODS

_____

_____

_____

_____

_____

_____

_____

_____

_____

_____

_____

_____

_____

_____

_____

_____

_____

_____

LEVEL OF WASTE: ◯ ◯ ◯ ◯ ◯

GARDEN NOTES

GARDEN NOTES

PLANT NAME	DATE PLANTED

WATER REQUIREMENTS   SUNLIGHT

SEED   TRANSPLANT

Date	Event

NOTES

OUTCOME

USES

PURCHASED AT: PRICE

GARDEN NOTES

PLANT NAME	DATE PLANTED

WATER REQUIREMENTS

SUNLIGHT

SEED

TRANSPLANT

Date	Event

NOTES

OUTCOME

USES

PURCHASED AT:

PRICE

GARDEN NOTES

PLANT NAME	DATE PLANTED

WATER REQUIREMENTS   SUNLIGHT

SEED   TRANSPLANT

Date	Event

NOTES

OUTCOME

USES

PURCHASED AT: PRICE

GARDEN NOTES

PLANT NAME	DATE PLANTED

WATER REQUIREMENTS

SUNLIGHT

SEED

TRANSPLANT

Date	Event

NOTES

OUTCOME

USES

PURCHASED AT:

PRICE

Zero waste habit tracker

ZERO WASTE HABIT TRACKER

MONTH   YEAR

Day															
1															
2															
3															
4															
5															
6															
7															
8															
9															
10															
11															
12															
13															
14															
15															
16															
17															
18															
19															
20															
21															
22															
23															
24															
25															
26															
27															
28															
29															
30															
31															

ZERO WASTE HABIT TRACKER

MONTH   YEAR

Day														
1														
2														
3														
4														
5														
6														
7														
8														
9														
10														
11														
12														
13														
14														
15														
16														
17														
18														
19														
20														
21														
22														
23														
24														
25														
26														
27														
28														
29														
30														
31														

ZERO WASTE HABIT TRACKER

Day														
1														
2														
3														
4														
5														
6														
7														
8														
9														
10														
11														
12														
13														
14														
15														
16														
17														
18														
19														
20														
21														
22														
23														
24														
25														
26														
27														
28														
29														
30														
31														

ZERO WASTE HABIT TRACKER

MONTH   YEAR

Day														
1														
2														
3														
4														
5														
6														
7														
8														
9														
10														
11														
12														
13														
14														
15														
16														
17														
18														
19														
20														
21														
22														
23														
24														
25														
26														
27														
28														
29														
30														
31														

ZERO WASTE HABIT TRACKER

MONTH   YEAR

Day														
1														
2														
3														
4														
5														
6														
7														
8														
9														
10														
11														
12														
13														
14														
15														
16														
17														
18														
19														
20														
21														
22														
23														
24														
25														
26														
27														
28														
29														
30														
31														

ZERO WASTE HABIT TRACKER

Month

Year

Day															
1															
2															
3															
4															
5															
6															
7															
8															
9															
10															
11															
12															
13															
14															
15															
16															
17															
18															
19															
20															
21															
22															
23															
24															
25															
26															
27															
28															
29															
30															
31															

ZERO WASTE HABIT TRACKER

Month   Year

Day														
1														
2														
3														
4														
5														
6														
7														
8														
9														
10														
11														
12														
13														
14														
15														
16														
17														
18														
19														
20														
21														
22														
23														
24														
25														
26														
27														
28														
29														
30														
31														

Zero waste habit tracker

Month   Year

Day															
1															
2															
3															
4															
5															
6															
7															
8															
9															
10															
11															
12															
13															
14															
15															
16															
17															
18															
19															
20															
21															
22															
23															
24															
25															
26															
27															
28															
29															
30															
31															

ZERO WASTE HABIT TRACKER

MONTH   YEAR

Day														
1														
2														
3														
4														
5														
6														
7														
8														
9														
10														
11														
12														
13														
14														
15														
16														
17														
18														
19														
20														
21														
22														
23														
24														
25														
26														
27														
28														
29														
30														
31														

Zero waste habit tracker

Day														
1														
2														
3														
4														
5														
6														
7														
8														
9														
10														
11														
12														
13														
14														
15														
16														
17														
18														
19														
20														
21														
22														
23														
24														
25														
26														
27														
28														
29														
30														
31														

ZERO WASTE HABIT TRACKER

MONTH _____   YEAR _____

DAY

Day														
1														
2														
3														
4														
5														
6														
7														
8														
9														
10														
11														
12														
13														
14														
15														
16														
17														
18														
19														
20														
21														
22														
23														
24														
25														
26														
27														
28														
29														
30														
31														

ZERO WASTE HABIT TRACKER

MONTH

YEAR

DAY

Day														
1														
2														
3														
4														
5														
6														
7														
8														
9														
10														
11														
12														
13														
14														
15														
16														
17														
18														
19														
20														
21														
22														
23														
24														
25														
26														
27														
28														
29														
30														
31														

MONTHLY AND WEEKLY PLANNER

2020

January

S	M	T	W	T	F	S
			1	2	3	4
5	6	7	8	9	10	11
12	13	14	15	16	17	18
19	20	21	22	23	24	25
26	27	28	29	30	31	

February

S	M	T	W	T	F	S
						1
2	3	4	5	6	7	8
9	10	11	12	13	14	15
16	17	18	19	20	21	22
23	24	25	26	27	28	29

March

S	M	T	W	T	F	S
1	2	3	4	5	6	7
8	9	10	11	12	13	14
15	16	17	18	19	20	21
22	23	24	25	26	27	28
29	30	31				

April

S	M	T	W	T	F	S
			1	2	3	4
5	6	7	8	9	10	11
12	13	14	15	16	17	18
19	20	21	22	23	24	25
26	27	28	29	30		

May

S	M	T	W	T	F	S
					1	2
3	4	5	6	7	8	9
10	11	12	13	14	15	16
17	18	19	20	21	22	23
24	25	26	27	28	29	30
31						

June

S	M	T	W	T	F	S
	1	2	3	4	5	6
7	8	9	10	11	12	13
14	15	16	17	18	19	20
21	22	23	24	25	26	27
28	29	30				

July

S	M	T	W	T	F	S
			1	2	3	4
5	6	7	8	9	10	11
12	13	14	15	16	17	18
19	20	21	22	23	24	25
26	27	28	29	30	31	

August

S	M	T	W	T	F	S
						1
2	3	4	5	6	7	8
9	10	11	12	13	14	15
16	17	18	19	20	21	22
23	24	25	26	27	28	29
30	31					

September

S	M	T	W	T	F	S
		1	2	3	4	5
6	7	8	9	10	11	12
13	14	15	16	17	18	19
20	21	22	23	24	25	26
27	28	29	30			

October

S	M	T	W	T	F	S
				1	2	3
4	5	6	7	8	9	10
11	12	13	14	15	16	17
18	19	20	21	22	23	24
25	26	27	28	29	30	31

November

S	M	T	W	T	F	S
1	2	3	4	5	6	7
8	9	10	11	12	13	14
15	16	17	18	19	20	21
22	23	24	25	26	27	28
29	30					

December

S	M	T	W	T	F	S
		1	2	3	4	5
6	7	8	9	10	11	12
13	14	15	16	17	18	19
20	21	22	23	24	25	26
27	28	29	30	31		

2021

January

S	M	T	W	T	F	S
					1	2
3	4	5	6	7	8	9
10	11	12	13	14	15	16
17	18	19	20	21	22	23
24	25	26	27	28	29	30
31						

February

S	M	T	W	T	F	S
	1	2	3	4	5	6
7	8	9	10	11	12	13
14	15	16	17	18	19	20
21	22	23	24	25	26	27
28						

March

S	M	T	W	T	F	S
	1	2	3	4	5	6
7	8	9	10	11	12	13
14	15	16	17	18	19	20
21	22	23	24	25	26	27
28	29	30	31			

April

S	M	T	W	T	F	S
				1	2	3
4	5	6	7	8	9	10
11	12	13	14	15	16	17
18	19	20	21	22	23	24
25	26	27	28	29	30	

May

S	M	T	W	T	F	S
						1
2	3	4	5	6	7	8
9	10	11	12	13	14	15
16	17	18	19	20	21	22
23	24	25	26	27	28	29
30	31					

June

S	M	T	W	T	F	S
		1	2	3	4	5
6	7	8	9	10	11	12
13	14	15	16	17	18	19
20	21	22	23	24	25	26
27	28	29	30			

July

S	M	T	W	T	F	S
				1	2	3
4	5	6	7	8	9	10
11	12	13	14	15	16	17
18	19	20	21	22	23	24
25	26	27	28	29	30	31

August

S	M	T	W	T	F	S
1	2	3	4	5	6	7
8	9	10	11	12	13	14
15	16	17	18	19	20	21
22	23	24	25	26	27	28
29	30	31				

September

S	M	T	W	T	F	S
			1	2	3	4
5	6	7	8	9	10	11
12	13	14	15	16	17	18
19	20	21	22	23	24	25
26	27	28	29	30		

October

S	M	T	W	T	F	S
					1	2
3	4	5	6	7	8	9
10	11	12	13	14	15	16
17	18	19	20	21	22	23
24	25	26	27	28	29	30
31						

November

S	M	T	W	T	F	S
	1	2	3	4	5	6
7	8	9	10	11	12	13
14	15	16	17	18	19	20
21	22	23	24	25	26	27
28	29	30				

December

S	M	T	W	T	F	S
			1	2	3	4
5	6	7	8	9	10	11
12	13	14	15	16	17	18
19	20	21	22	23	24	25
26	27	28	29	30	31	

2022

January

S	M	T	W	T	F	S
						1
2	3	4	5	6	7	8
9	10	11	12	13	14	15
16	17	18	19	20	21	22
23	24	25	26	27	28	29
30	31					

February

S	M	T	W	T	F	S
		1	2	3	4	5
6	7	8	9	10	11	12
13	14	15	16	17	18	19
20	21	22	23	24	25	26
27	28					

March

S	M	T	W	T	F	S
		1	2	3	4	5
6	7	8	9	10	11	12
13	14	15	16	17	18	19
20	21	22	23	24	25	26
27	28	29	30	31		

April

S	M	T	W	T	F	S
					1	2
3	4	5	6	7	8	9
10	11	12	13	14	15	16
17	18	19	20	21	22	23
24	25	26	27	28	29	30

May

S	M	T	W	T	F	S
1	2	3	4	5	6	7
8	9	10	11	12	13	14
15	16	17	18	19	20	21
22	23	24	25	26	27	28
29	30	31				

June

S	M	T	W	T	F	S
			1	2	3	4
5	6	7	8	9	10	11
12	13	14	15	16	17	18
19	20	21	22	23	24	25
26	27	28	29	30		

July

S	M	T	W	T	F	S
					1	2
3	4	5	6	7	8	9
10	11	12	13	14	15	16
17	18	19	20	21	22	23
24	25	26	27	28	29	30
31						

August

S	M	T	W	T	F	S
	1	2	3	4	5	6
7	8	9	10	11	12	13
14	15	16	17	18	19	20
21	22	23	24	25	26	27
28	29	30	31			

September

S	M	T	W	T	F	S
				1	2	3
4	5	6	7	8	9	10
11	12	13	14	15	16	17
18	19	20	21	22	23	24
25	26	27	28	29	30	

October

S	M	T	W	T	F	S
						1
2	3	4	5	6	7	8
9	10	11	12	13	14	15
16	17	18	19	20	21	22
23	24	25	26	27	28	29
30	31					

November

S	M	T	W	T	F	S
		1	2	3	4	5
6	7	8	9	10	11	12
13	14	15	16	17	18	19
20	21	22	23	24	25	26
27	28	29	30			

December

S	M	T	W	T	F	S
				1	2	3
4	5	6	7	8	9	10
11	12	13	14	15	16	17
18	19	20	21	22	23	24
25	26	27	28	29	30	31

January 2021

Sunday	Monday	Tuesday	Wednesday	Thursday	Friday	Saturday
27	28	29	30	31	1	2
3	4	5	6	7	8	9
10	11	12	13	14	15	16
17	18	19	20	21	22	23
24	25	26	27	28	29	30
31	1	2	3	4	5	6

February 2021

Sunday	Monday	Tuesday	Wednesday	Thursday	Friday	Saturday
31	1	2	3	4	5	6
7	8	9	10	11	12	13
14	15	16	17	18	19	20
21	22	23	24	25	26	27
28	1	2	3	4	5	6

March 2021

Sunday	Monday	Tuesday	Wednesday	Thursday	Friday	Saturday
28	1	2	3	4	5	6
7	8	9	10	11	12	13
14	15	16	17	18	19	20
21	22	23	24	25	26	27
28	29	30	31	1	2	3

April 2021

Sunday	Monday	Tuesday	Wednesday	Thursday	Friday	Saturday
28	29	30	31	1	2	3
4	5	6	7	8	9	10
11	12	13	14	15	16	17
18	19	20	21	22	23	24
25	26	27	28	29	30	1

May 2021

Sunday	Monday	Tuesday	Wednesday	Thursday	Friday	Saturday
25	26	27	28	29	30	1
2	3	4	5	6	7	8
9	10	11	12	13	14	15
16	17	18	19	20	21	22
23	24	25	26	27	28	29
30	31	1	2	3	4	5

June 2021

Sunday	Monday	Tuesday	Wednesday	Thursday	Friday	Saturday
30	31	1	2	3	4	5
6	7	8	9	10	11	12
13	14	15	16	17	18	19
20	21	22	23	24	25	26
27	28	29	30	1	2	3

July 2021

Sunday	Monday	Tuesday	Wednesday	Thursday	Friday	Saturday
27	28	29	30	1	2	3
4	5	6	7	8	9	10
11	12	13	14	15	16	17
18	19	20	21	22	23	24
25	26	27	28	29	30	31

August 2021

Sunday	Monday	Tuesday	Wednesday	Thursday	Friday	Saturday
1	2	3	4	5	6	7
8	9	10	11	12	13	14
15	16	17	18	19	20	21
22	23	24	25	26	27	28
29	30	31	1	2	3	4

September 2021

Sunday	Monday	Tuesday	Wednesday	Thursday	Friday	Saturday
29	30	31	1	2	3	4
5	6	7	8	9	10	11
12	13	14	15	16	17	18
19	20	21	22	23	24	25
26	27	28	29	30	1	2

October 2021

Sunday	Monday	Tuesday	Wednesday	Thursday	Friday	Saturday
26	27	28	29	30	1	2
3	4	5	6	7	8	9
10	11	12	13	14	15	16
17	18	19	20	21	22	23
24	25	26	27	28	29	30
31	1	2	3	4	5	6

November 2021

Sunday	Monday	Tuesday	Wednesday	Thursday	Friday	Saturday
31	1	2	3	4	5	6
7	8	9	10	11	12	13
14	15	16	17	18	19	20
21	22	23	24	25	26	27
28	29	30	1	2	3	4

December 2021

Sunday	Monday	Tuesday	Wednesday	Thursday	Friday	Saturday
28	29	30	1	2	3	4
5	6	7	8	9	10	11
12	13	14	15	16	17	18
19	20	21	22	23	24	25
26	27	28	29	30	31	1

December

○ 7. MONDAY

ZERO WASTE ACTIONS

○ 8. TUESDAY

○ 9. WEDNESDAY

TO DO

○ 10. THURSDAY

○ 11. FRIDAY

○ 12. SATURDAY / 13. SUNDAY

December

○ 14. MONDAY

ZERO WASTE ACTIONS

○ 15. TUESDAY

○ 16. WEDNESDAY

TO DO

○ 17. THURSDAY

○ 18. FRIDAY

○ 19. SATURDAY / 20. SUNDAY

December

○ 21. MONDAY

ZERO WASTE ACTIONS

○ 22. TUESDAY

○ 23. WEDNESDAY

TO DO

○ 24. THURSDAY

○ 25. FRIDAY

○ 26. SATURDAY / 27. SUNDAY

December

○ 28. MONDAY

ZERO WASTE ACTIONS

○ 29. TUESDAY

○ 30. WEDNESDAY

TO DO

○ 31. THURSDAY

○ 1. FRIDAY

○ 2. SATURDAY / 3. SUNDAY

January

○ 4. MONDAY

ZERO WASTE ACTIONS

○ 5. TUESDAY

○ 6. WEDNESDAY

TO DO

○ 7. THURSDAY

○ 8. FRIDAY

○ 9. SATURDAY / 10. SUNDAY

January

○ 11. MONDAY

ZERO WASTE ACTIONS

○ 12. TUESDAY

○ 13. WEDNESDAY

TO DO

○ 14. THURSDAY

○ 15. FRIDAY

○ 16. SATURDAY / 17. SUNDAY

January

○ 18. MONDAY

ZERO WASTE ACTIONS

○ 19. TUESDAY

○ 20. WEDNESDAY

TO DO

○ 21. THURSDAY

○ 22. FRIDAY

○ 23. SATURDAY / 24. SUNDAY

January

○ 25. MONDAY

ZERO WASTE ACTIONS

○ 26. TUESDAY

○ 27. WEDNESDAY

TO DO

○ 28. THURSDAY

○ 29. FRIDAY

○ 30. SATURDAY / 31. SUNDAY

February

○ 1. MONDAY

ZERO WASTE ACTIONS

○ 2. TUESDAY

○ 3. WEDNESDAY

TO DO

○ 4. THURSDAY

○ 5. FRIDAY

○ 6. SATURDAY / 7. SUNDAY

February

02/08/21 - 02/14/21

○ 8. MONDAY

○ 9. TUESDAY

○ 10. WEDNESDAY

○ 11. THURSDAY

○ 12. FRIDAY

○ 13. SATURDAY / 14. SUNDAY

ZERO WASTE ACTIONS

TO DO

February

○ 15. MONDAY

ZERO WASTE ACTIONS

○ 16. TUESDAY

○ 17. WEDNESDAY

TO DO

○ 18. THURSDAY

○ 19. FRIDAY

○ 20. SATURDAY / 21. SUNDAY

February

○ 22. MONDAY

ZERO WASTE ACTIONS

○ 23. TUESDAY

○ 24. WEDNESDAY

TO DO

○ 25. THURSDAY

○ 26. FRIDAY

○ 27. SATURDAY / 28. SUNDAY

March

○ 1. MONDAY

○ 2. TUESDAY

○ 3. WEDNESDAY

○ 4. THURSDAY

○ 5. FRIDAY

○ 6. SATURDAY / 7. SUNDAY

ZERO WASTE ACTIONS

TO DO

March

○ 8. MONDAY

ZERO WASTE ACTIONS

○ 9. TUESDAY

○ 10. WEDNESDAY

TO DO

○ 11. THURSDAY

○ 12. FRIDAY

○ 13. SATURDAY / 14. SUNDAY

March

○ 15. MONDAY

ZERO WASTE ACTIONS

○ 16. TUESDAY

○ 17. WEDNESDAY

TO DO

○ 18. THURSDAY

○ 19. FRIDAY

○ 20. SATURDAY / 21. SUNDAY

March

03/22/21 - 03/28/21

○ 22. MONDAY

ZERO WASTE ACTIONS

○ 23. TUESDAY

○ 24. WEDNESDAY

TO DO

○ 25. THURSDAY

○ 26. FRIDAY

○ 27. SATURDAY / 28. SUNDAY

March

03/29/21 - 04/04/21

○ 29. MONDAY

ZERO WASTE ACTIONS

○ 30. TUESDAY

○ 31. WEDNESDAY

TO DO

○ 1. THURSDAY

○ 2. FRIDAY

○ 3. SATURDAY / 4. SUNDAY

April

○ 5. MONDAY

ZERO WASTE ACTIONS

○ 6. TUESDAY

○ 7. WEDNESDAY

TO DO

○ 8. THURSDAY

○ 9. FRIDAY

○ 10. SATURDAY / 11. SUNDAY

April

04/12/21 - 04/18/21

○ 12. MONDAY

ZERO WASTE ACTIONS

○ 13. TUESDAY

○ 14. WEDNESDAY

TO DO

○ 15. THURSDAY

○ 16. FRIDAY

○ 17. SATURDAY / 18. SUNDAY

April

○ 19. MONDAY

ZERO WASTE ACTIONS

○ 20. TUESDAY

○ 21. WEDNESDAY

TO DO

○ 22. THURSDAY

○ 23. FRIDAY

○ 24. SATURDAY / 25. SUNDAY

April

○ 26. MONDAY

ZERO WASTE ACTIONS

○ 27. TUESDAY

○ 28. WEDNESDAY

TO DO

○ 29. THURSDAY

○ 30. FRIDAY

○ 1. SATURDAY / 2. SUNDAY

May

○ 3. MONDAY

ZERO WASTE ACTIONS

○ 4. TUESDAY

○ 5. WEDNESDAY

TO DO

○ 6. THURSDAY

○ 7. FRIDAY

○ 8. SATURDAY / 9. SUNDAY

May

○ 10. MONDAY

ZERO WASTE ACTIONS

○ 11. TUESDAY

○ 12. WEDNESDAY

TO DO

○ 13. THURSDAY

○ 14. FRIDAY

○ 15. SATURDAY / 16. SUNDAY

May

○ 17. MONDAY

ZERO WASTE ACTIONS

○ 18. TUESDAY

○ 19. WEDNESDAY

TO DO

○ 20. THURSDAY

○ 21. FRIDAY

○ 22. SATURDAY / 23. SUNDAY

May

○ 24. MONDAY

ZERO WASTE ACTIONS

○ 25. TUESDAY

○ 26. WEDNESDAY

TO DO

○ 27. THURSDAY

○ 28. FRIDAY

○ 29. SATURDAY / 30. SUNDAY

May

○ 31. MONDAY

ZERO WASTE ACTIONS

○ 1. TUESDAY

○ 2. WEDNESDAY

TO DO

○ 3. THURSDAY

○ 4. FRIDAY

○ 5. SATURDAY / 6. SUNDAY

June

○ 7. MONDAY

ZERO WASTE ACTIONS

○ 8. TUESDAY

○ 9. WEDNESDAY

TO DO

○ 10. THURSDAY

○ 11. FRIDAY

○ 12. SATURDAY / 13. SUNDAY

June

06/14/21 - 06/20/21

○ 14. MONDAY

ZERO WASTE ACTIONS

○ 15. TUESDAY

○ 16. WEDNESDAY

TO DO

○ 17. THURSDAY

○ 18. FRIDAY

○ 19. SATURDAY / 20. SUNDAY

June

○ 21. MONDAY

ZERO WASTE ACTIONS

○ 22. TUESDAY

○ 23. WEDNESDAY

TO DO

○ 24. THURSDAY

○ 25. FRIDAY

○ 26. SATURDAY / 27. SUNDAY

June

○ 28. MONDAY

ZERO WASTE ACTIONS

○ 29. TUESDAY

○ 30. WEDNESDAY

TO DO

○ 1. THURSDAY

○ 2. FRIDAY

○ 3. SATURDAY / 4. SUNDAY

July

○ 5. MONDAY

ZERO WASTE ACTIONS

○ 6. TUESDAY

○ 7. WEDNESDAY

TO DO

○ 8. THURSDAY

○ 9. FRIDAY

○ 10. SATURDAY / 11. SUNDAY

July

07/12/21 - 07/18/21

○ 12. MONDAY

ZERO WASTE ACTIONS

○ 13. TUESDAY

○ 14. WEDNESDAY

TO DO

○ 15. THURSDAY

○ 16. FRIDAY

○ 17. SATURDAY / 18. SUNDAY

July

○ 19. MONDAY

ZERO WASTE ACTIONS

○ 20. TUESDAY

○ 21. WEDNESDAY

TO DO

○ 22. THURSDAY

○ 23. FRIDAY

○ 24. SATURDAY / 25. SUNDAY

July

○ 26. MONDAY

ZERO WASTE ACTIONS

○ 27. TUESDAY

○ 28. WEDNESDAY

TO DO

○ 29. THURSDAY

○ 30. FRIDAY

○ 31. SATURDAY / 1. SUNDAY

August

○ 2. MONDAY

○ 3. TUESDAY

○ 4. WEDNESDAY

○ 5. THURSDAY

○ 6. FRIDAY

○ 7. SATURDAY / 8. SUNDAY

ZERO WASTE ACTIONS

TO DO

August

○ 9. MONDAY

ZERO WASTE ACTIONS

○ 10. TUESDAY

○ 11. WEDNESDAY

TO DO

○ 12. THURSDAY

○ 13. FRIDAY

○ 14. SATURDAY / 15. SUNDAY

August

○ 16. MONDAY

ZERO WASTE ACTIONS

○ 17. TUESDAY

○ 18. WEDNESDAY

TO DO

○ 19. THURSDAY

○ 20. FRIDAY

○ 21. SATURDAY / 22. SUNDAY

August

○ 23. MONDAY

○ 24. TUESDAY

○ 25. WEDNESDAY

○ 26. THURSDAY

○ 27. FRIDAY

○ 28. SATURDAY / 29. SUNDAY

ZERO WASTE ACTIONS

TO DO

August

○ 30. MONDAY

ZERO WASTE ACTIONS

○ 31. TUESDAY

○ 1. WEDNESDAY

TO DO

○ 2. THURSDAY

○ 3. FRIDAY

○ 4. SATURDAY / 5. SUNDAY

September

○ 6. MONDAY

ZERO WASTE ACTIONS

○ 7. TUESDAY

○ 8. WEDNESDAY

TO DO

○ 9. THURSDAY

○ 10. FRIDAY

○ 11. SATURDAY / 12. SUNDAY

September

○ 13. MONDAY

ZERO WASTE ACTIONS

○ 14. TUESDAY

○ 15. WEDNESDAY

TO DO

○ 16. THURSDAY

○ 17. FRIDAY

○ 18. SATURDAY / 19. SUNDAY

September

○ 20. MONDAY

ZERO WASTE ACTIONS

○ 21. TUESDAY

○ 22. WEDNESDAY

TO DO

○ 23. THURSDAY

○ 24. FRIDAY

○ 25. SATURDAY / 26. SUNDAY

September

○ 27. MONDAY

ZERO WASTE ACTIONS

○ 28. TUESDAY

○ 29. WEDNESDAY

TO DO

○ 30. THURSDAY

○ 1. FRIDAY

○ 2. SATURDAY / 3. SUNDAY

October

○ 4. MONDAY

ZERO WASTE ACTIONS

○ 5. TUESDAY

○ 6. WEDNESDAY

TO DO

○ 7. THURSDAY

○ 8. FRIDAY

○ 9. SATURDAY / 10. SUNDAY

October

10/11/21 - 10/17/21

○ 11. MONDAY

ZERO WASTE ACTIONS

○ 12. TUESDAY

○ 13. WEDNESDAY

TO DO

○ 14. THURSDAY

○ 15. FRIDAY

○ 16. SATURDAY / 17. SUNDAY

October

○ 18. MONDAY

ZERO WASTE ACTIONS

○ 19. TUESDAY

○ 20. WEDNESDAY

TO DO

○ 21. THURSDAY

○ 22. FRIDAY

○ 23. SATURDAY / 24. SUNDAY

October

10/25/21 - 10/31/21

○ 25. MONDAY

ZERO WASTE ACTIONS

○ 26. TUESDAY

○ 27. WEDNESDAY

TO DO

○ 28. THURSDAY

○ 29. FRIDAY

○ 30. SATURDAY / 31. SUNDAY

November

○ 1. MONDAY

ZERO WASTE ACTIONS

○ 2. TUESDAY

○ 3. WEDNESDAY

TO DO

○ 4. THURSDAY

○ 5. FRIDAY

○ 6. SATURDAY / 7. SUNDAY

November

○ 8. MONDAY

ZERO WASTE ACTIONS

○ 9. TUESDAY

○ 10. WEDNESDAY

TO DO

○ 11. THURSDAY

○ 12. FRIDAY

○ 13. SATURDAY / 14. SUNDAY

November

○ 15. MONDAY

ZERO WASTE ACTIONS

○ 16. TUESDAY

○ 17. WEDNESDAY

TO DO

○ 18. THURSDAY

○ 19. FRIDAY

○ 20. SATURDAY / 21. SUNDAY

November

○ 22. MONDAY

ZERO WASTE ACTIONS

○ 23. TUESDAY

○ 24. WEDNESDAY

TO DO

○ 25. THURSDAY

○ 26. FRIDAY

○ 27. SATURDAY / 28. SUNDAY

November

○ 29. MONDAY

ZERO WASTE ACTIONS

○ 30. TUESDAY

○ 1. WEDNESDAY

TO DO

○ 2. THURSDAY

○ 3. FRIDAY

○ 4. SATURDAY / 5. SUNDAY

December

12/06/21 - 12/12/21

○ 6. MONDAY

ZERO WASTE ACTIONS

○ 7. TUESDAY

○ 8. WEDNESDAY

TO DO

○ 9. THURSDAY

○ 10. FRIDAY

○ 11. SATURDAY / 12. SUNDAY

December

○ 13. MONDAY

○ 14. TUESDAY

○ 15. WEDNESDAY

○ 16. THURSDAY

○ 17. FRIDAY

○ 18. SATURDAY / 19. SUNDAY

ZERO WASTE ACTIONS

TO DO

December

○ 20. MONDAY

○ 21. TUESDAY

○ 22. WEDNESDAY

○ 23. THURSDAY

○ 24. FRIDAY

○ 25. SATURDAY / 26. SUNDAY

ZERO WASTE ACTIONS

TO DO

December

○ 27. MONDAY

ZERO WASTE ACTIONS

○ 28. TUESDAY

○ 29. WEDNESDAY

TO DO

○ 30. THURSDAY

○ 31. FRIDAY

○ 1. SATURDAY / 2. SUNDAY

Printed in Great Britain
by Amazon